Leela can Sk

by Alison Hawes

illustrated by Carol Yoshizumi

I can put on my skates.

I can stand up on my skates.

I can run on my skates.

I can spin on my skates.

I can jump on my skates.

10

I can't stop on my skates.

Help!

14

Leela can Skate 🐾 Alison Hawes

Teaching notes written by Sue Bodman and Glen Franklin

Using this book

Developing reading comprehension

Leela is learning to skate. But she can't stop. Simple language structures are used repetitively to explain what she can and can't do on her skates. Pictures provide good support for the text meaning.

Grammar and sentence structure

- Text is well-spaced to support the development of one-to-one correspondence.
- The changes to two lines of text on pages 12-13, providing good support for early experiences of return sweep onto a new line of text.
- In contexts where children are learning English as an additional language, support by rehearsing the sentence structures orally before introducing the book.

Word meaning and spelling

- Check vocabulary predictions by looking at the first letter of each action ('jump', 'run', 'hop', 'stand up').
- Rehearse blending easy to hear sounds into a familiar word 'can', 'run'.
- Reinforce recognition of frequently occurring words 'put', 'on', 'my'.

Curriculum links

PSHE – Leela wears shin pads, knee pads and a helmet throughout. Why does she wear them? What other play activities do the children need to wear protective clothing to do?

Science – Explore a selection of everyday objects to find out which can roll. Grouping and sorting activities would support discussion and practical investigations. Why do they roll? Do they have particular spatial properties?

Learning Outcomes

Children can:

- understand that print carries meaning and is read from left to right, top to bottom
- read some high-frequency words and use phonic knowledge to work out some simple words
- show an understanding of a sequence of events.

A guided reading lesson

Book Introduction

Give a book to each child and read the title.

Orientation

Give a brief orientation to the text: Leela is learning to skate. This story tells us about all the things she can do.

Preparation

Page 2: Leela is getting ready to skate. Her brother doesn't have to help her. (indicate her brother in the picture) Do you think it is tricky to put on skates? How do you know?

Page 4: Leela can stand up. She says 'I can stand up on my skates.' Let's all practise pointing carefully to each word as we read. Demonstrate by holding your book so the children can see you track. Then check that each child tracks each word accurately. Support if necessary.

Page 6: What else can Leela do? Yes, she can run on her skates. Let's practise pointing to each word carefully. Support if the slightly modified language structure means that some of the children find it difficult to track one-to-one.